This bite-sized book h
a useful overview of h
help you to achieve th

- ✓ Understand your ⟨...⟩ emotional decisio⟨...⟩
- ✓ Create perspective and weigh up your options
- ✓ Substantiate your decision with relevant information
- ✓ Be confident about taking risks
- ✓ Adopt a growth mindset and learn from experience

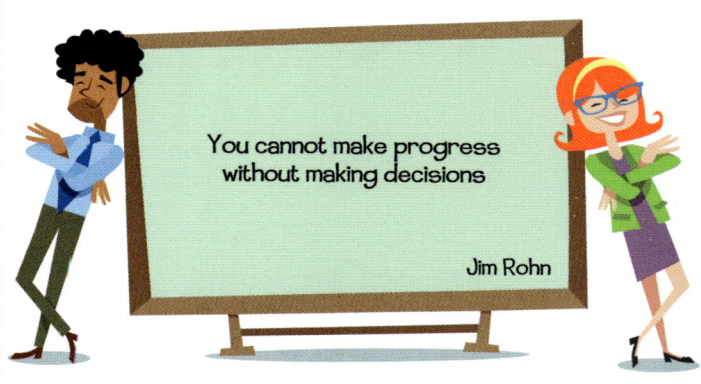

What is decision-making?

Decision-making is the cognitive process of making choices between different options. It involves identifying a problem or an opportunity, gathering information, evaluating options and finally selecting a course of action. The decision-making process can be influenced by a variety of factors including personal biases, emotions, what information we have available and time constraints.

Effective decision-making is a highly valuable skill for so many different aspects of our lives. It can help us navigate challenges and achieve our goals, as well as having an impact on our overall wellbeing because sometimes making decisions can be a stressful experience. The better able we are to make decisions, the more in control we will feel, and this can help boost our confidence and resilience. Regularly engaging in thoughtful decision-making can also strengthen our analytical and problem-solving abilities.

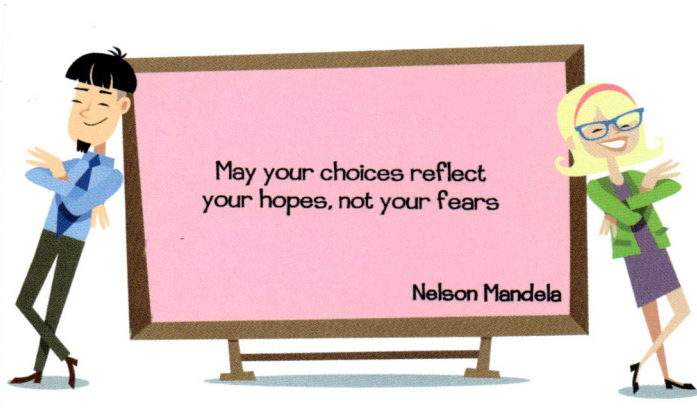

Overcoming obstacles

Decision-making can be hindered by a multitude of obstacles including cognitive biases that cloud our judgement, a lack of clear information or an overwhelming amount of information that leads to analysis paralysis. Other obstacles may include stress, fatigue, conflict, time constraints and pressure from other people that force us into making rushed decisions. We may well worry that we will make a mistake by making a wrong decision in the face of uncertainty and this can fuel fear and anxiety.

Overcoming these obstacles requires self-awareness, structured approaches and a willingness to consider diverse perspectives, as well as clarifying our goals and reviewing our options. It also helps to acknowledge that not every decision we make will be the best decision, risks may be taken, and mistakes will inevitably be made. This, however, is part of life's varied and imperfect journey and every outcome will provide us with an opportunity to learn and grow from the experience.

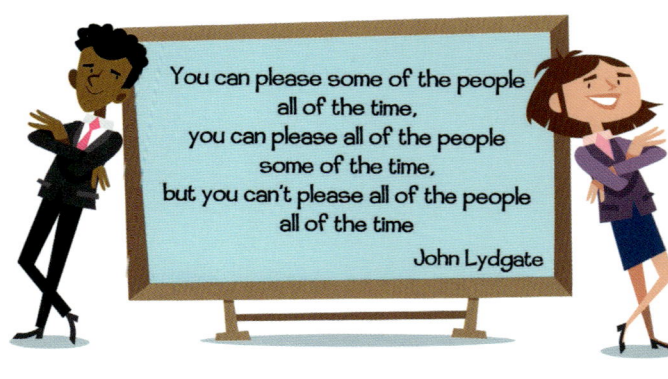

People pleasing

It is completely understandable to worry about what other people think when we make decisions, and it is a natural human tendency to want to be liked and accepted. However, when this worry starts to dictate our choices and cause us stress, it's time to take a step back and consider a different approach. It also helps to appreciate that no matter what we do we will not please everyone all the time.

Often, our worries about what other people think can be based on assumptions rather than reality. We may even be projecting our own insecurities and thoughts onto others because a lot of the time we don't even know what is going on in someone else's mind. It helps to remind ourselves that we simply can't control other people's thoughts or opinions; however, we can control our own responses and decisions.

Stress and wellbeing

Let's face it, sometimes making decisions can be a stressful experience. Dealing with choices can be a significant source of stress and anxiety, especially when there is a lot of change and uncertainty going on. Being an assertive decision-maker will equip us with the tools and mindset to navigate these situations with greater ease. By taking a proactive and structured approach to decision-making, we will be able to gain a sense of control over challenging situations and choices.

This feeling of confidence and control can reduce the fear of uncertainty, leading to lower stress levels and improved overall wellbeing. Knowing we can confidently tackle decisions empowers us to face challenges head-on rather than feeling overwhelmed and stressed by them.

Boosting confidence

The experience of making well-reasoned and successful decisions can build a strong sense of self-belief and confidence. Each positive outcome reinforces trust in our own judgement, making future decision-making processes smoother and more confident. This growth in confidence can also act as a buffer against 'analysis paralysis' – the state of overthinking that prevents action.

When we gather sufficient information, evaluate it effectively and act decisively, it can help us to feel empowered. It is important that we also focus on extracting lessons from the decisions we make that don't always work out as well as we would have liked and view them as an opportunity for growth. This, in turn, builds resilience and future confidence in our decision-making abilities.

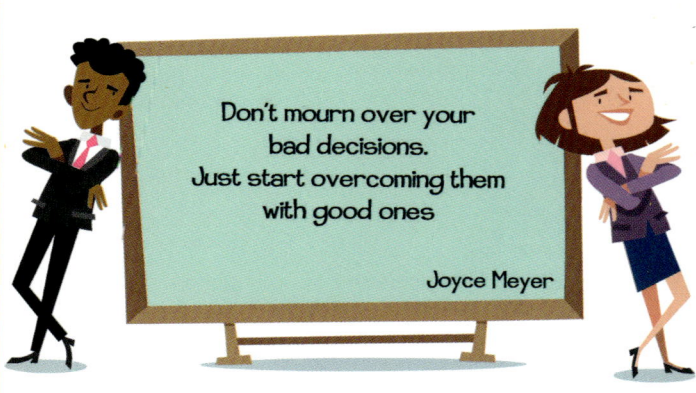

Procrastination

Decision-making and procrastination are often intertwined, creating a cycle that stops us from getting things done. The act of postponing decision-making is known as decisional procrastination, and this can stem from fear of making the wrong choices or simply feeling overwhelmed by the options available to us.

The fear of making a bad decision is a significant driver of procrastination. It can create a cycle where the anxiety of potential negative outcomes leads to avoidance, which only delays the inevitable decision and often increases our stress levels. So, instead of viewing decisions as either 'good' or 'bad', it can help to shift our perspective and see them as opportunities for experimentation, learning and growth. Even if an outcome isn't what we had hoped for, we can always gain valuable experience and information for future decisions.

THE EISENHOWER DECISION MATRIX

	Urgent	Not Urgent
Important	DO — Do it now	DECIDE — Schedule a time to do it
Not Important	DELEGATE — Who can do it for you?	DELETE — Eliminate it

The Eisenhower Decision Matrix was developed by Dwight D. Eisenhower and is a simple and powerful tool for prioritising tasks based on their urgency and importance. It can help us to identify what truly matters and distinguish between what needs immediate attention and what can be planned. It will also help us to focus our energy on high-impact activities and reduce the feeling of being overwhelmed by a long to-do list.

The Eisenhower Decision Matrix cont.

Urgent and important – These are the tasks we should tackle immediately and could be deadlines or problems that need our direct attention.

Important and not urgent – These tasks are crucial for our long-term goals and should be scheduled in for later. This is where we need to focus our time to prevent things from becoming urgent. This could be planning, learning new skills, or building relationships.

Urgent and not important – These tasks demand our attention; however, they don't contribute significantly to our goals. If possible, it is better to delegate them to someone else. This could be meetings, interruptions or requests that don't directly involve our key responsibilities.

Neither urgent nor important – These are tasks that are mostly distractions and should be avoided or eliminated altogether and are likely time-wasting activities.

By using this matrix, we can make conscious decisions about how we spend our time and energy, leading to greater productivity and less stress.

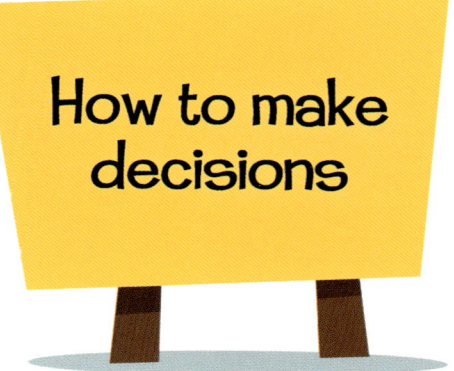

Clearly define your decision

Clearly defining a decision and identifying exactly what we are hoping to achieve is the first step in any effective decision-making process. Without clarity, the next steps of gathering information, evaluating options and making a final choice could become unfocused. Investing time in clearly defining the decision and desired outcome upfront will save us significant effort and potential confusion.

A precise definition acts as a compass, guiding the entire decision-making process and if we are involving other people this is essential for shared understanding of what we are trying to achieve. Articulating or even writing down (in the simplest terms possible) exactly what the decision is and why it needs to be made is a good place to start.

Keep calm

Keeping as calm and relaxed as possible when we are making decisions will help us to think more clearly, focus our attention and embrace a rational assessment of a situation. By managing our emotions, we can avoid impulsive reactions and make decisions based on logical analysis rather than emotional bias. This will lead us to more effective and well-informed decisions.

A calm mind allows for better concentration and the ability to process information thoroughly, leading to a clearer understanding of a situation and our available options. Deep breathing, mindfulness, progressive muscle relaxation and scheduling in time for relaxation can help us to feel calmer.

> Great decision-making comes from the ability to create the time and space to think rationally and intelligently about the issue at hand
>
> Graham Allcott

Take your time

When faced with a decision, it is helpful to take a deliberate pause. This could be as simple as taking a few deep breaths, stepping away from the situation for a moment and doing something else, or even sleeping on it if time permits. This time and space allows our initial emotional reaction to subside and provides us with the clarity to think more rationally and consider different perspectives.

Once we have created this initial space, we can also use the time to gather information and explore our options more thoroughly. In a fast-paced world we may even put pressure on ourselves to have all the answers right away. Building in time for careful consideration, even if it takes a little bit longer, can lead to a more sound and well-reasoned outcome.

Establish a clear criteria

To establish a clear criteria for our decision-making, we need to identify the core objectives we want to achieve with our decision. What are the essential outcomes we are hoping for? Listing factors that will influence whether a particular choice is successful or not in meeting those objectives is helpful, as these factors will form the basis of our criteria.

Once we have our initial list, we can refine it by prioritising the most important factors because not all criteria will carry the same weight. It can be worth ranking or categorising our criteria by referring to the Eisenhower Decision Matrix on page 14 to reflect on their significance. This will provide a framework for evaluating our options so we can make a more focused and well-considered decision.

Check your facts

When making important decisions, fact-checking is a crucial step to ensure we are basing our choices on accurate information and advice. We can start by identifying the sources of the information we are using and checking for reliability and credibility. We need to be aware of information from unknown or biased sources, including social media posts without clear origins.

When we come across conflicting information, it helps to apply critical-thinking skills and dig deeper to understand what is going on behind the scenes. Looking for evidence-based information is important and there are many fact-checking websites and tools designed to evaluate the accuracy of information. Advice from people around us can be presented with a particular slant, so it is helpful to check our facts and understand the context and potential biases of all our sources of information.

Consider potential biases

It most definitely helps to consider our potential biases when making decisions and to be aware of the common types of biases that can influence our thinking. These might include confirmation bias (seeking information that confirms existing beliefs), availability bias (relying on easily recalled information), or anchoring bias (over-relying on the first piece of information we receive). Recognising these tendencies in ourselves is important.

We need to actively challenge our initial assumptions and seek out diverse perspectives by asking ourselves if we are giving more weight to information that aligns with what we already believe. Raising our self-awareness and being open to feedback from others is essential for helping to identify our unconscious biases.

Seek out diverse perspectives

Seeking out different perspectives can inject a vital dose of reality and robustness into our decision-making process. Engaging with people who have different viewpoints helps us to actively challenge our own assumptions, which will broaden our understanding of the decision we are trying to make. This can help us identify potential blind spots, uncover unforeseen consequences and reveal innovative solutions that might have been missed if we had made the decision on our own.

The power of diverse perspectives lies in its ability to reduce biases and encourage well-rounded and inclusive decisions. When we actively seek out and consider a range of opinions, we move beyond the limitations of individual thinking and tap into a collective intelligence.

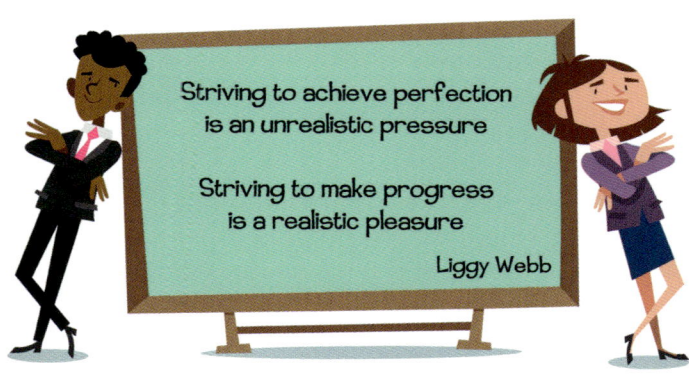

Challenge perfectionism

Perfectionism can cast a long shadow over the decision-making process, often leading to analysis paralysis. The relentless pursuit of making a flawless decision can trap us in an endless cycle of information gathering and evaluation. Fear of making the 'wrong' choice could become so overwhelming that we delay or even avoid making any decision at all.

To navigate this, it is helpful to consider that perfection is an illusion and that most decisions involve trade-offs and uncertainties. Setting realistic standards, accepting that mistakes are part of life, and focusing on progress rather than flawless outcomes can help to alleviate the pressure we may put ourselves under. If we are not careful, the 'super me' we try to be can stifle our ability to make timely decisions.

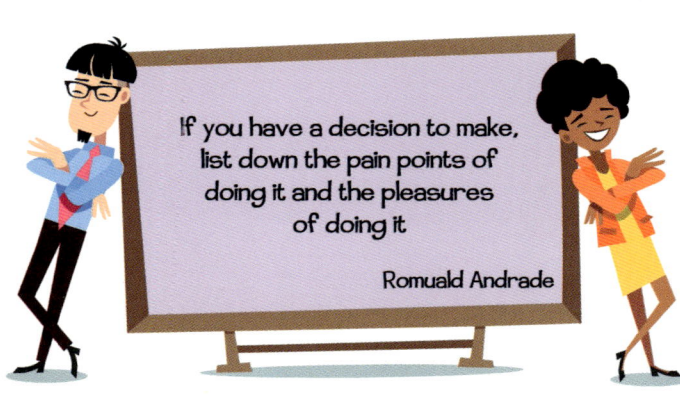

Weigh up cons and pros

Weighing up the pros and cons is a traditional and time-tested method and often effective step in the decision-making process. It involves systematically listing the potential advantages (pros) and disadvantages (cons) associated with each available option. This structured approach can help to bring clarity to the potential outcomes and allows for a more objective comparison between choices. It can also be more helpful to flip it the other way round and draw up a cons and pros list so we don't sabotage all the pros and end up focusing on all the cons.

By carefully considering both the negative and positive aspects of each option, we can gain a clearer understanding of the potential trade-offs involved. This process encourages a balanced perspective, moving beyond immediate emotional responses to a more rational evaluation of the potential consequences.

Ultimately, a well-thought-out cons and pros list can provide valuable insights to guide us towards a well-considered and confident decision.

Sleep on it

Sleeping on a decision (when possible) may offer significant benefits by allowing our subconscious mind to process information without the immediate pressure of conscious thought. During sleep, our brain continues to work on the problem, consolidating memories and making new connections. This can sometimes lead to fresh insights and a clearer perspective.

Taking a break overnight also helps us to detach emotionally from the immediate urgency of the decision. The clarity gained after a good night's rest can lead to a more confident and well-reasoned choice, as we approach the decision feeling refreshed and less emotionally charged.

Decision is a sharp knife
that cuts clean and straight;
indecision, a dull one that hacks
and tears and leaves ragged
edges behind it

Gordon Graham

Be assertive

Once we have carefully considered our options and made a decision, we need to be bold and stand firm in our choice. Assertiveness here means owning the choice we have made with confidence and conviction and not letting doubts chip away at our resolve. Once we have weighed things up, we need to act on our decision.

It is important to resist the temptation to dwell on the 'what ifs' because the path not taken is a landscape of endless possibilities, both positive and negative. Focusing on these hypotheticals can breed unnecessary anxiety and undermine our current course of action. Instead, we need to channel our energy into making the very best of our chosen path. We may well make some small adaptions along the way; however, we do need to keep moving forward and positively embrace the decision we have made.

Communicate your decision

When we communicate our decisions, we need to do this by clearly explaining the 'why' behind the decision and outlining the criteria and reasoning process that led to choices we have made. This helps to provide context and will also help other people to understand the basis of our decisions.

It is also important to clearly explain what actions will follow, who is responsible for these actions and any relevant timelines. We will also need to be prepared to answer questions and address any concerns. It may be that not everyone is happy with the decisions that we have made. However, if we have followed a rigorous and well-considered approach, we will be more likely to provide background information that will allay any concerns and encourage people to accept our decisions more confidently.

Learn from experience

Building in reflection time to review our decisions is an excellent use of our time because it can transform our experiences into profound learning opportunities. Reflection encourages a crucial element of self-awareness and helps us to identify our strengths and weaknesses by revealing recurring patterns of behaviour and blind spots that we might otherwise overlook.

By making reflection a regular practice, we can actively invest in our personal growth and development. This will help us to continuously learn from experience and fine-tune our ability to be better decision-makers going forward.

Summary

Here is a simple five-step approach to decision-making that summarises the content of this bite-sized book:

1. **Clearly define the decision** – Articulate and write down succinctly the problem you are trying to solve or the opportunity you are considering
2. **Gather information** – Collect relevant data and facts. Understand the situation, your options and potential constraints
3. **Consider your options** – Brainstorm and evaluate the possible choices available to you. What are the cons and pros/pros and cons of each option?
4. **Make the decision** – Based on your information and evaluation, choose the best option and take action
5. **Reflect and review** – After implementing your decision, take time to review the outcome and identify and embrace the lessons learnt from the experience

Recommended resources

These books and resources have been curated to help you to take a deeper dive into the concept of decision-making.

- ✓ Thinking, Fast and Slow – Daniel Kahneman
- ✓ How to Decide – Annie Duke
- ✓ The 6 Pillars of Decision Making – Patrik Ian Meyer
- ✓ Clear Thinking – Shane Parrish
- ✓ The Art of Decision Making – Joseph Bikart
- ✓ The Decision Book – Mikael Krogerus and Roman Tschäppeler
- ✓ Decisive – Chip and Dan Heath
- ✓ Critical Thinking – Liggy Webb

If you would like a free copy of the digital poster on page 38 please email: liggy@liggywebb.com

DECISION MAKING

How to make better choices

We are our choices

Jean-Paul Sartre

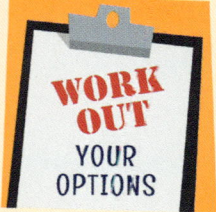

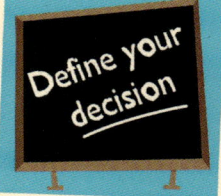

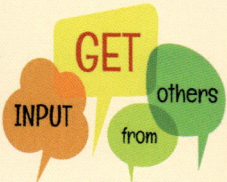

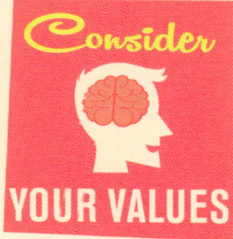

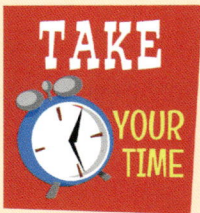

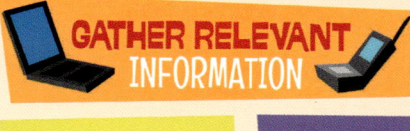

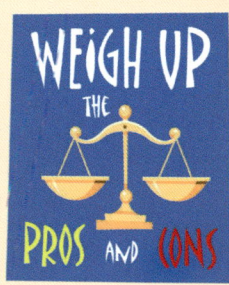

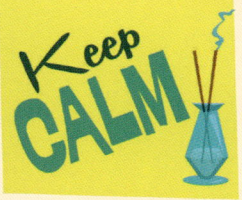

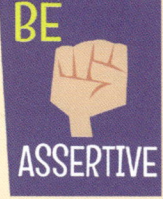